Colour to Calm
Serenity

"Serenity the state of being calm, peaceful, and untroubled."

by Anthony Falzon

www.colourtocalm.com

Copyright © 2016 Anthony Falzon

All rights reserved. No portion of this book may be reproduced mechanically, electronically or by any other means, including photocopying without written permission of the publisher.

Introduction

Hi, Anthony Falzon here, I just want to say thank you for purchasing my Adult colouring book.

I started to create adult colouring books due to the stress and strains modern life can bring and noticed how therapeutic it was to me in designing them as well as colouring them in.

I use to design and create by hand logo mats for shops, hotels, schools and other businesses that needed a logo mat in their foot wells!

I felt so relaxed and stress free designing and making these mats, that when I left (company relocated) to work for the NHS in mental health, I couldn't believe just how stress full my job would be from my last job!

I needed something to take away the stress I felt and after seeing colouring books used by the Occupational Therapists in classes and see them work, that's when I started creating my own adult colouring books for myself.

So... being an ex-skilled craftman, I decided to use my skills from the past to create these adult colouring books for all to use so you can see how colouring can be relaxing, calming and therapeutic.

Enjoy!

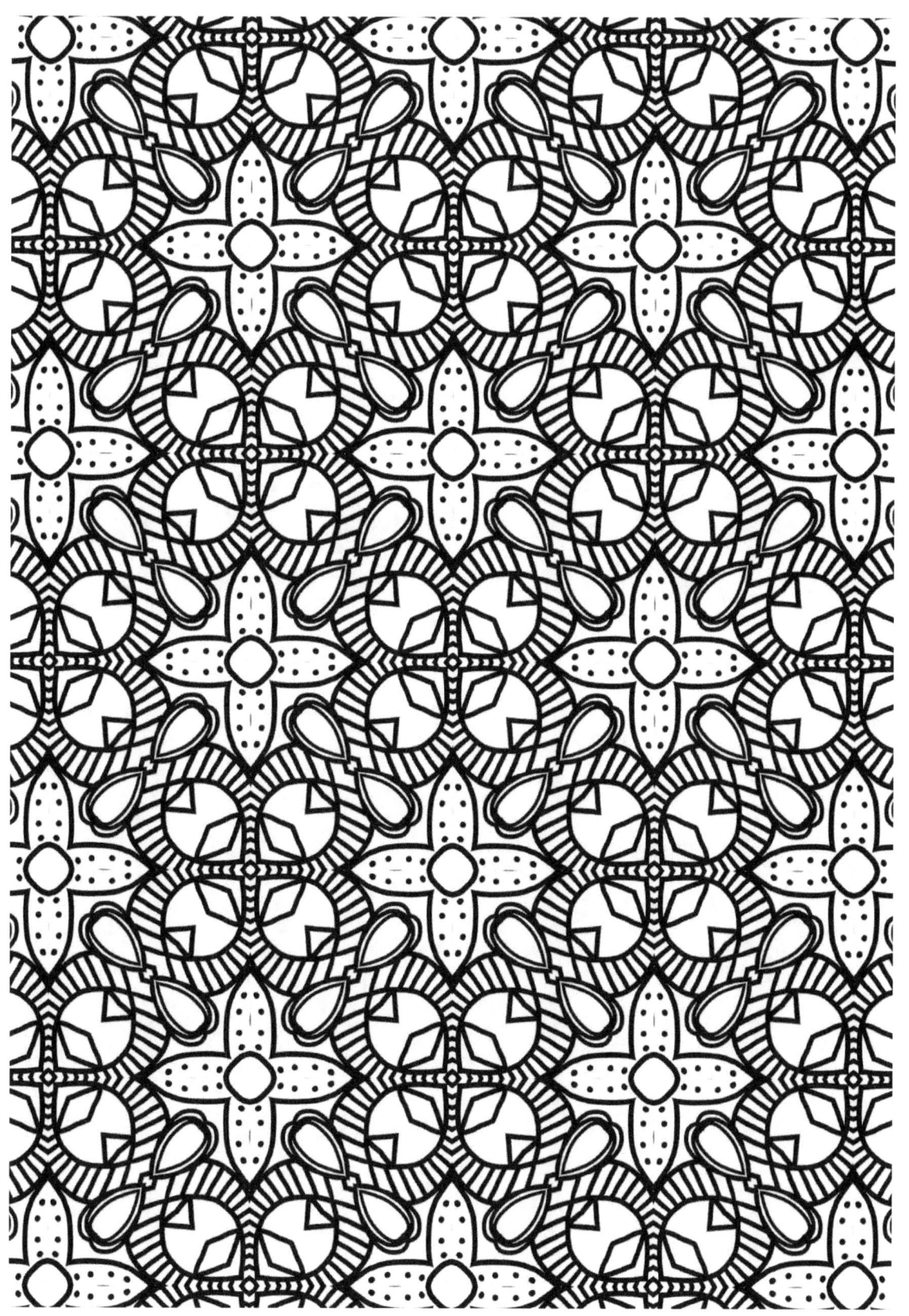

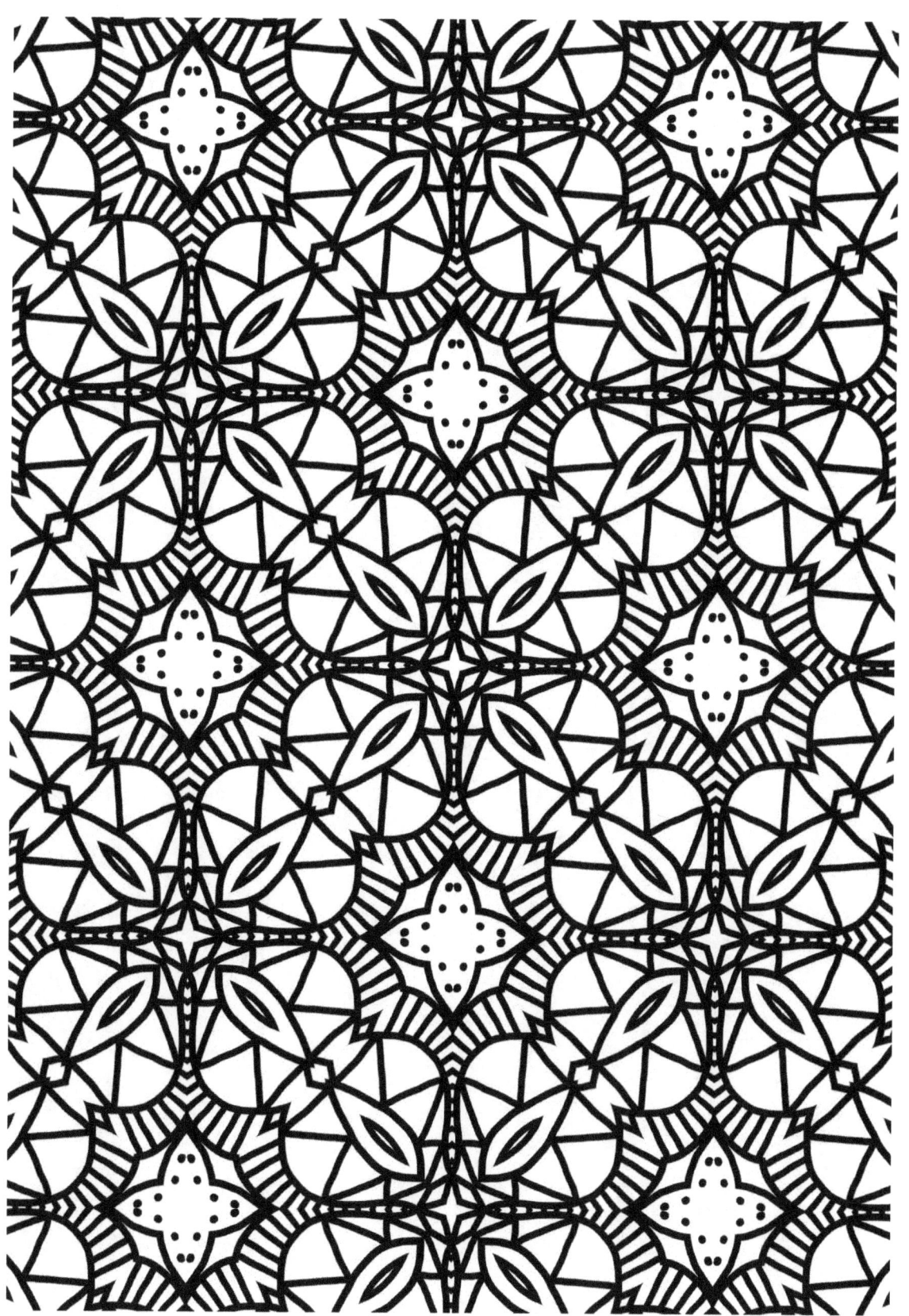

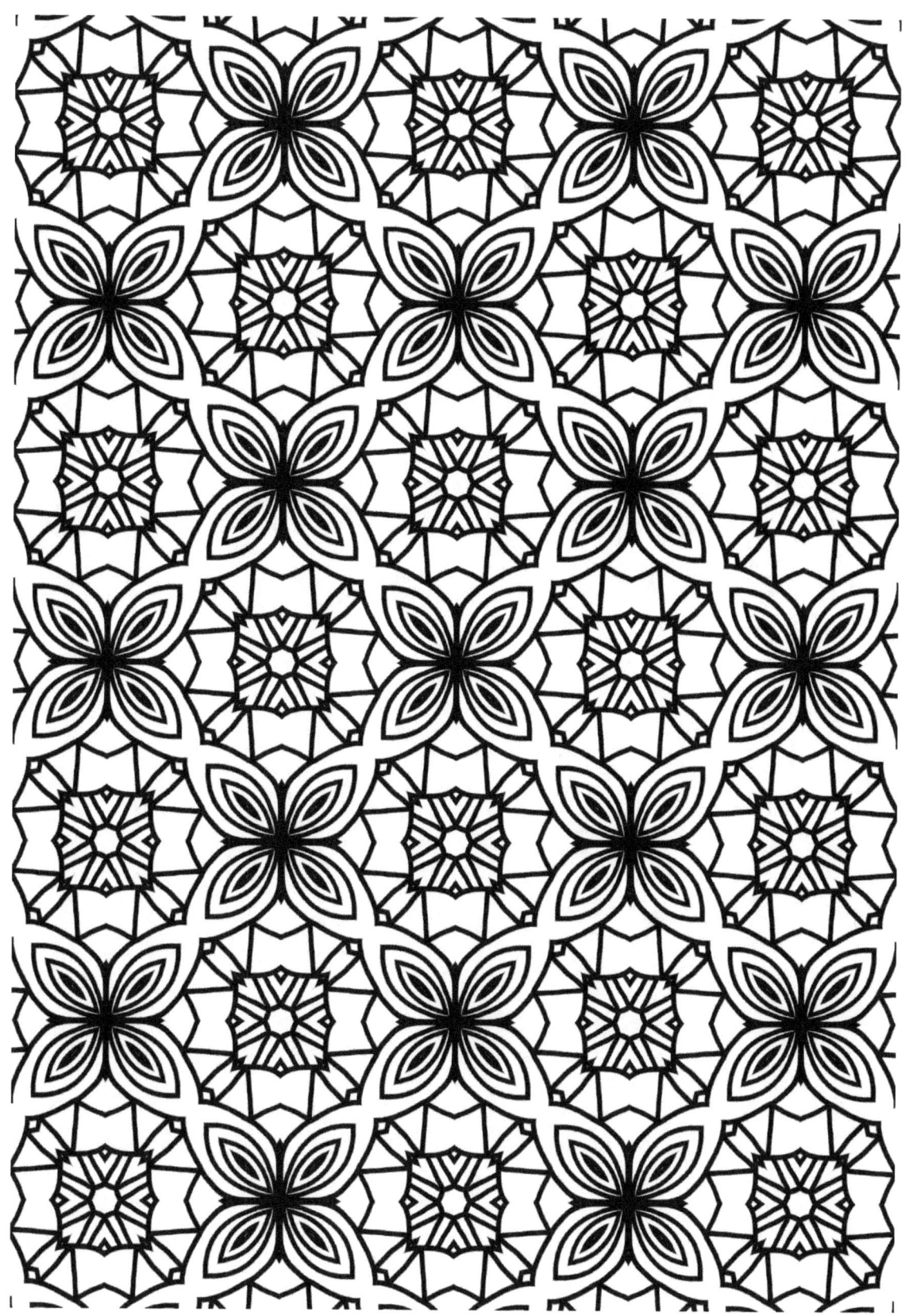

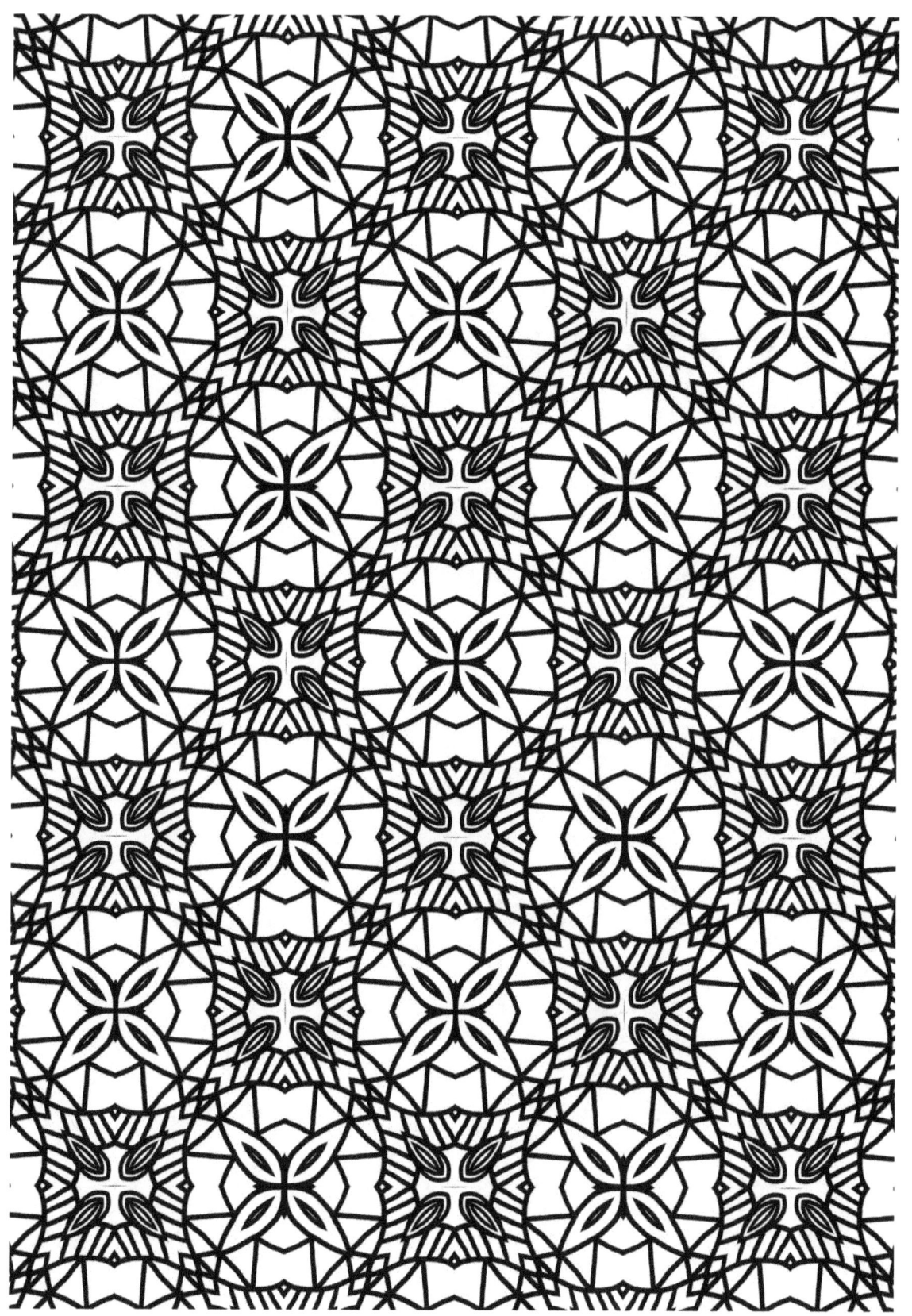

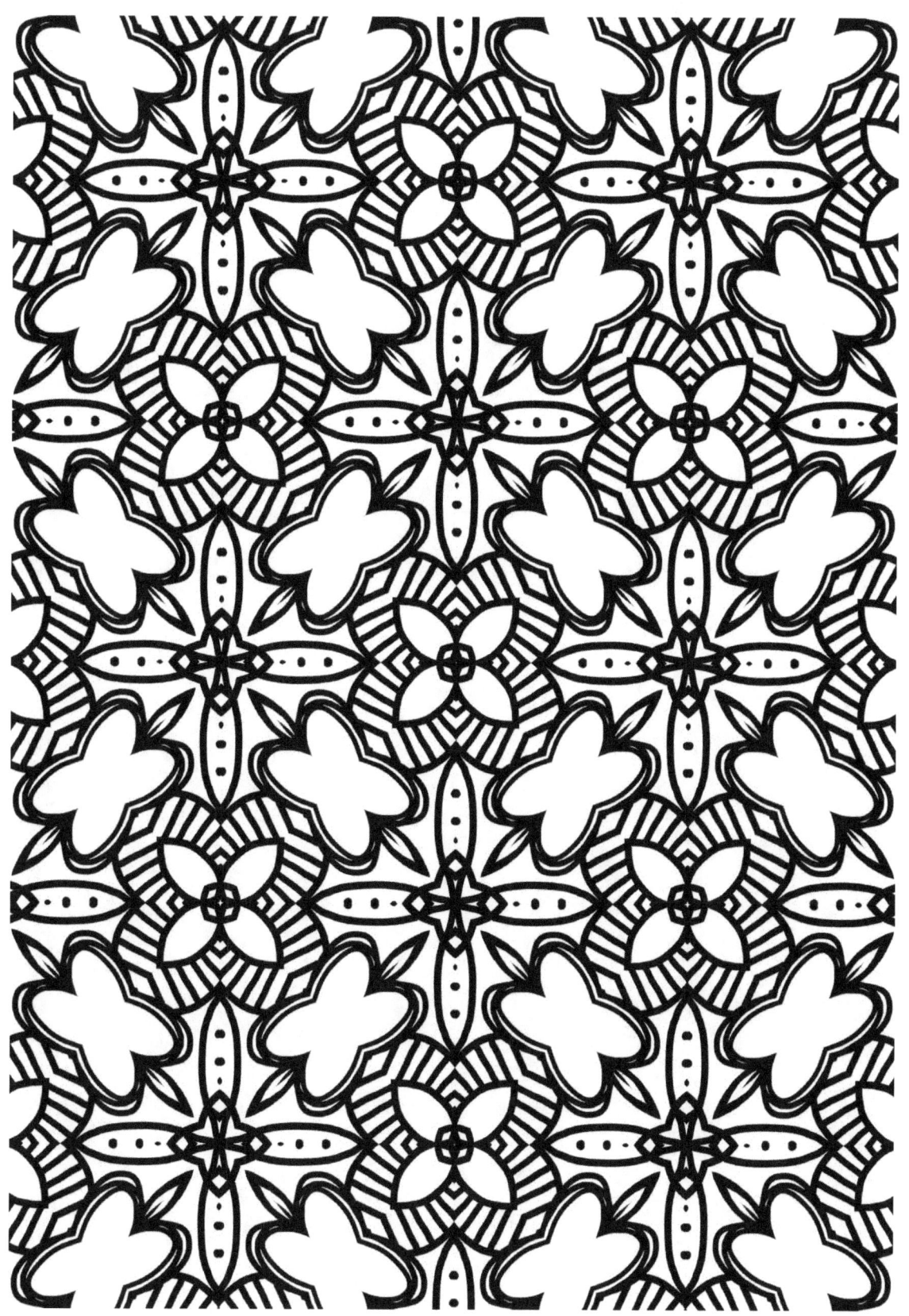

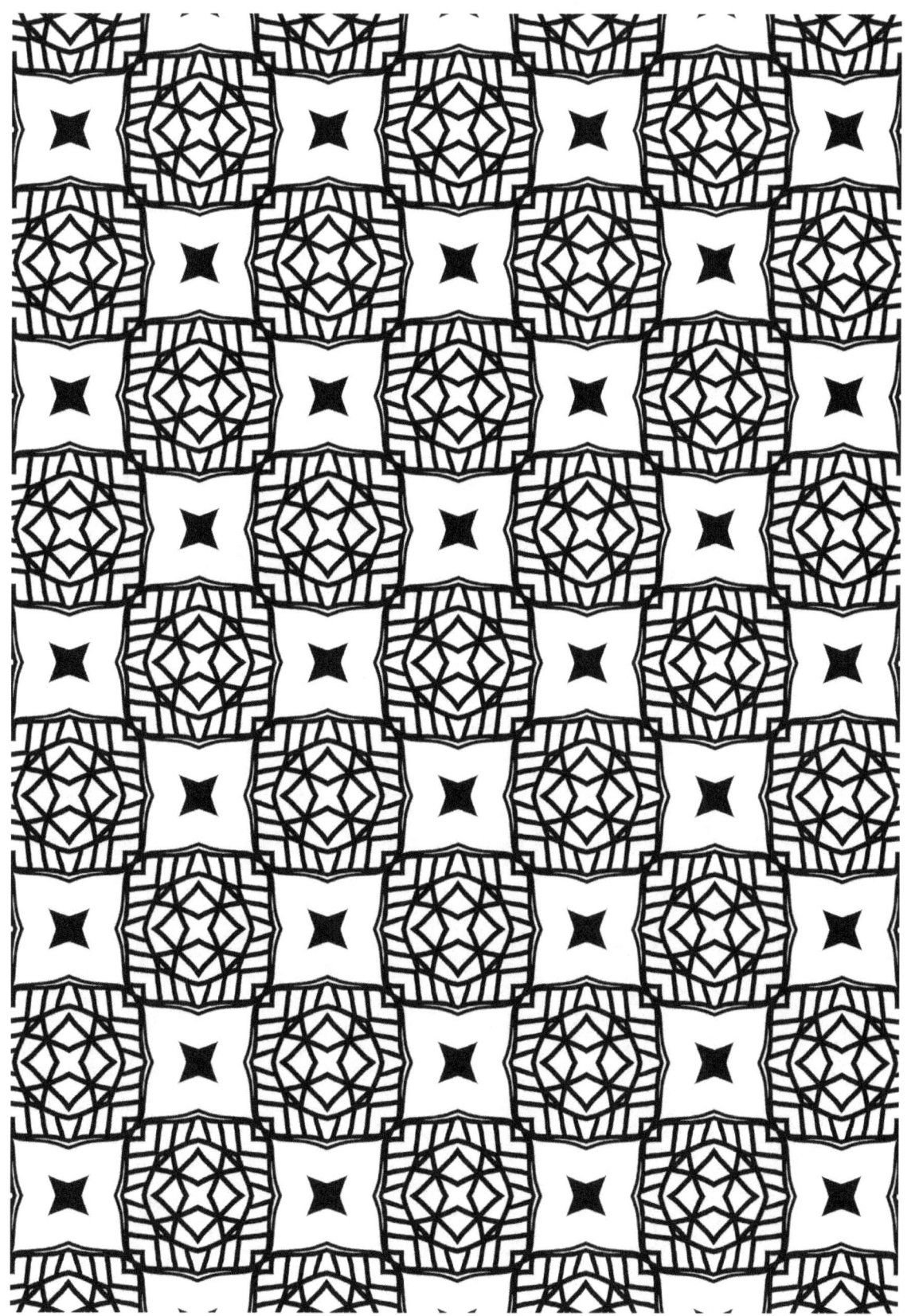

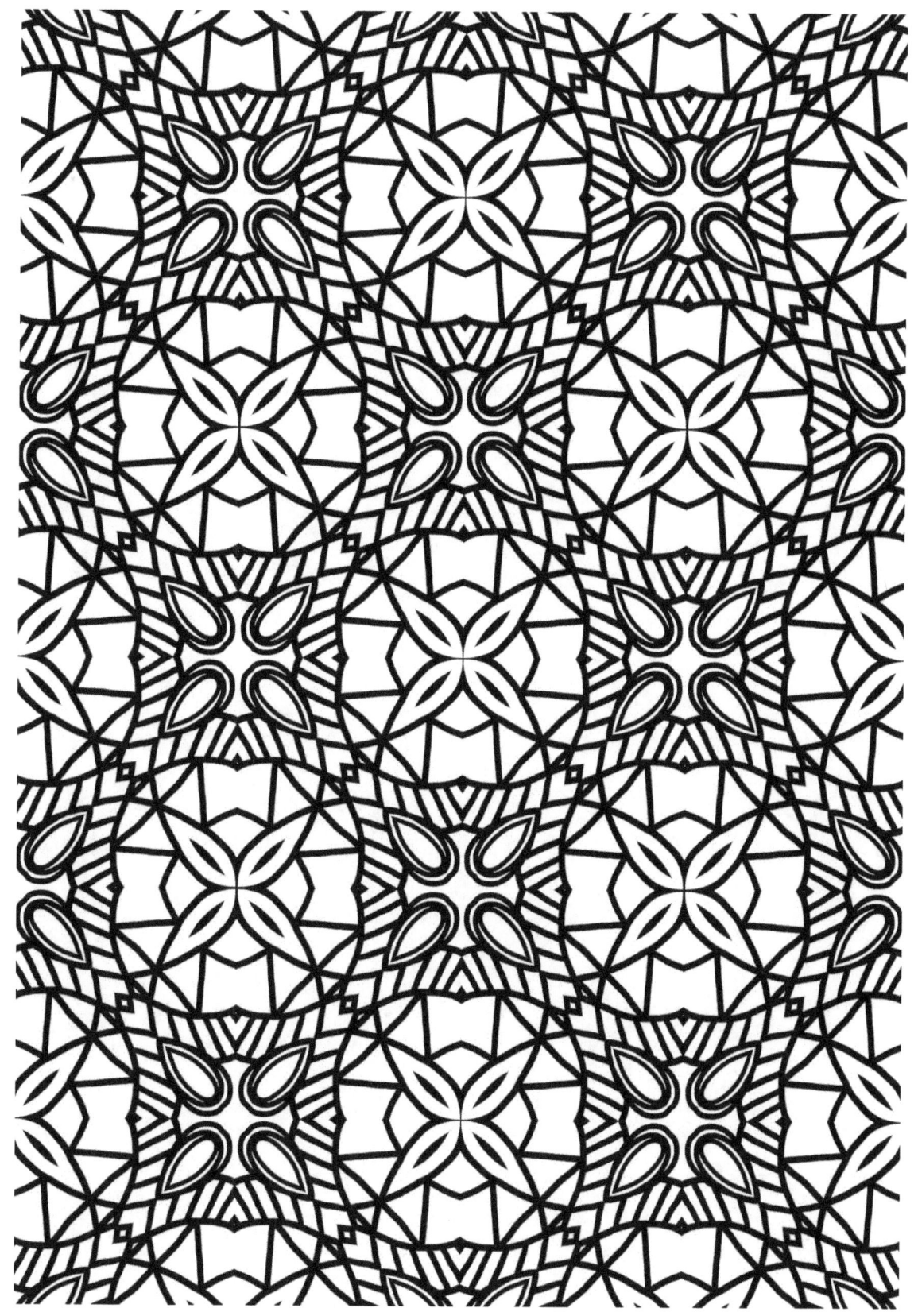

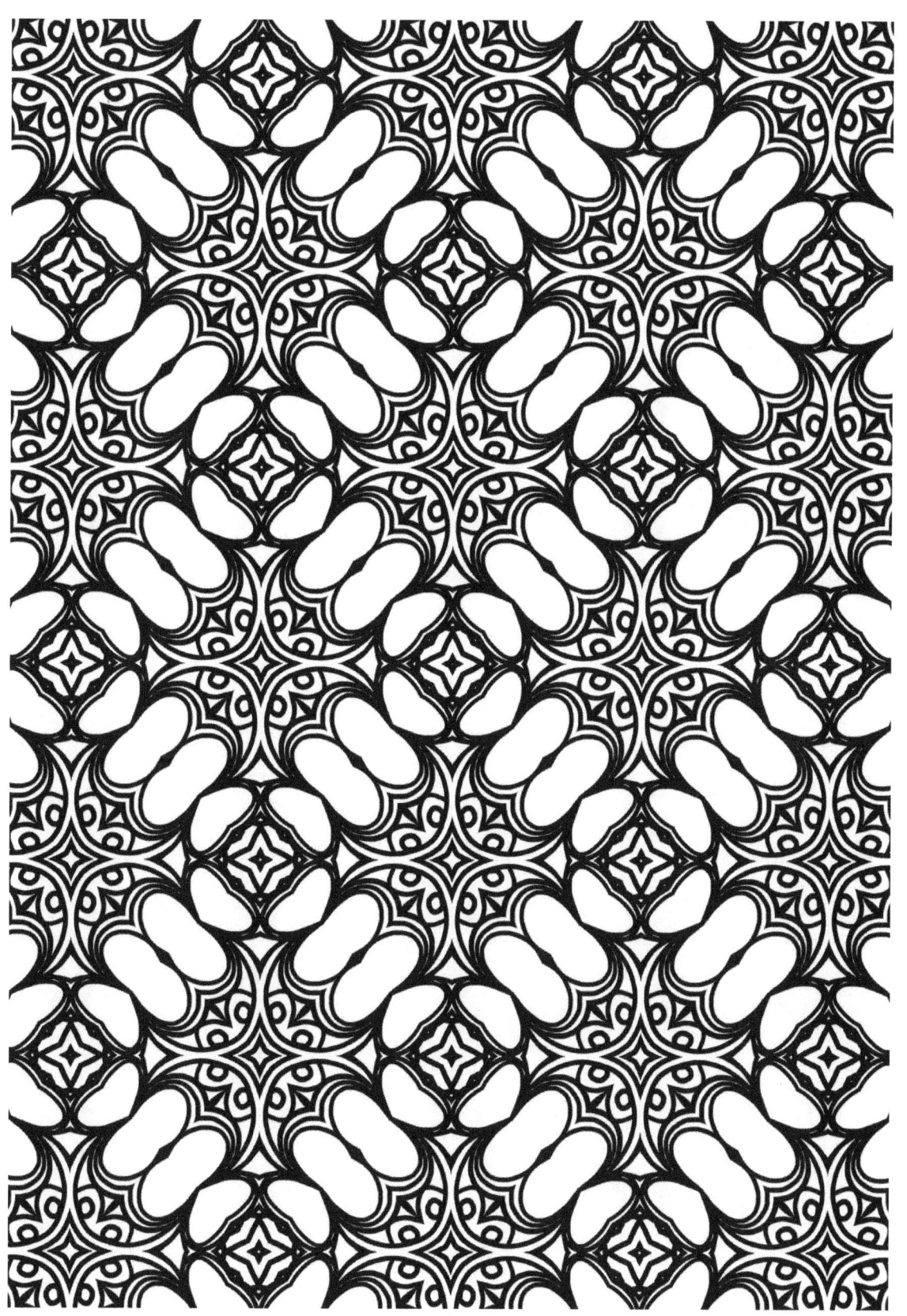

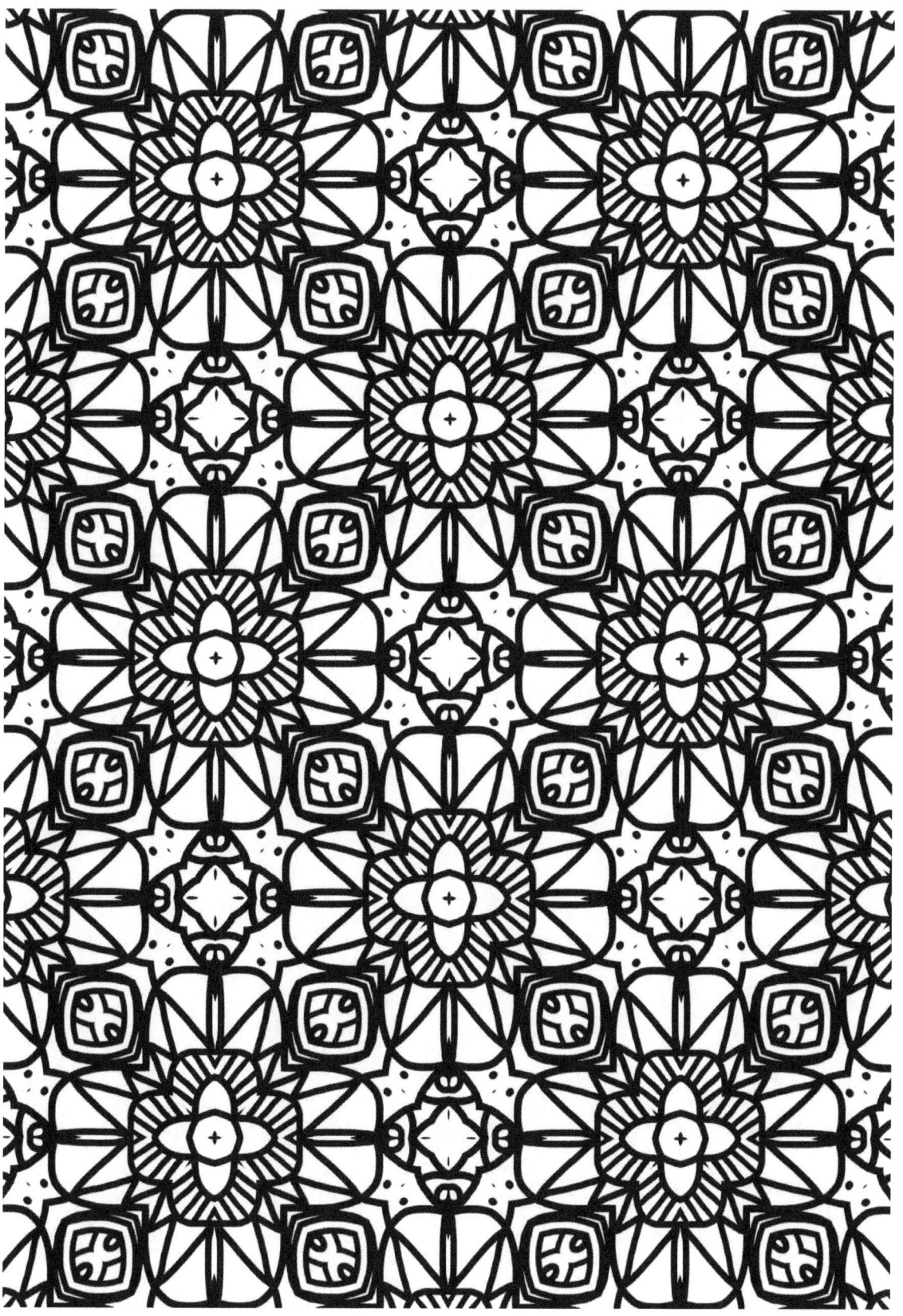

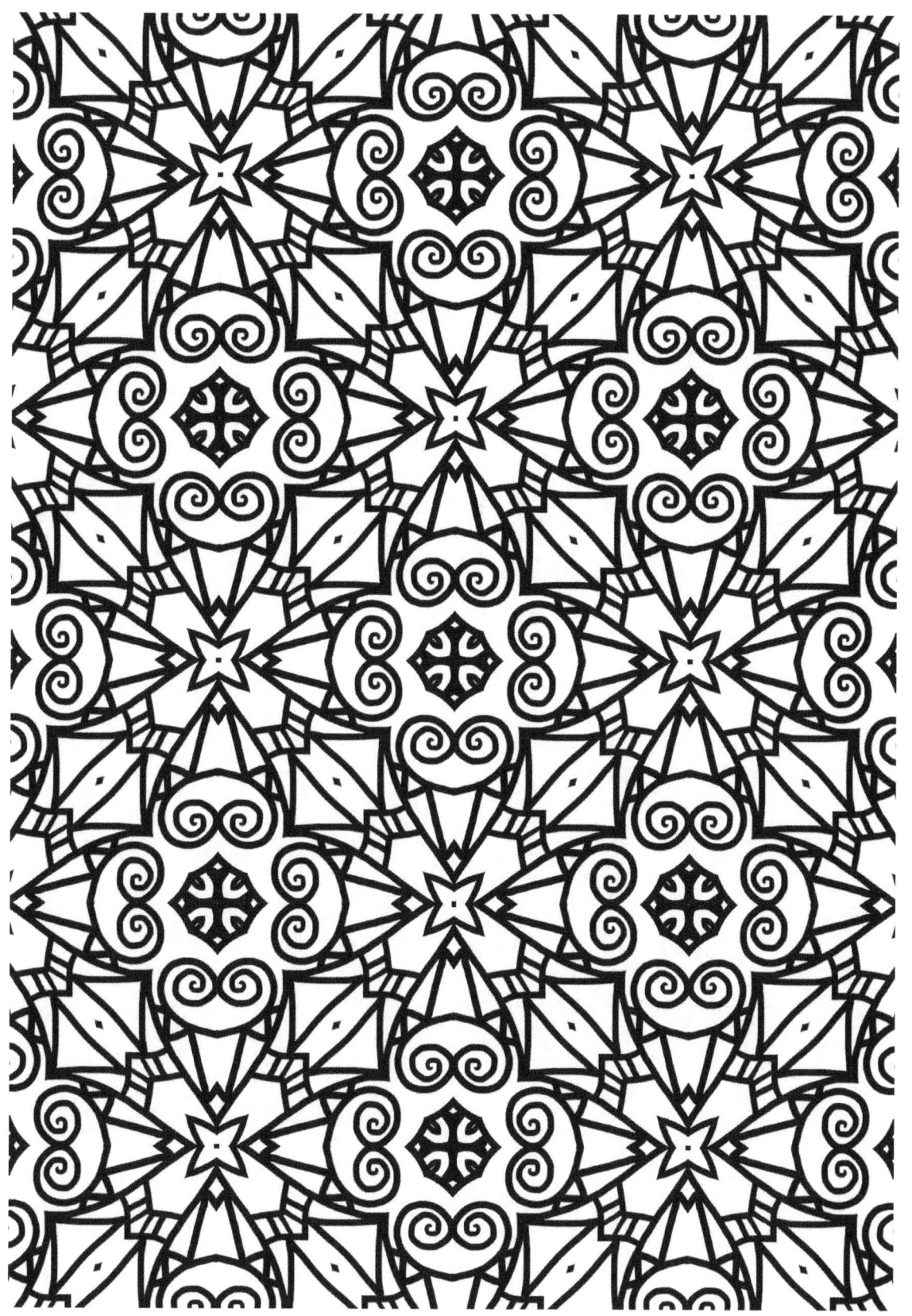

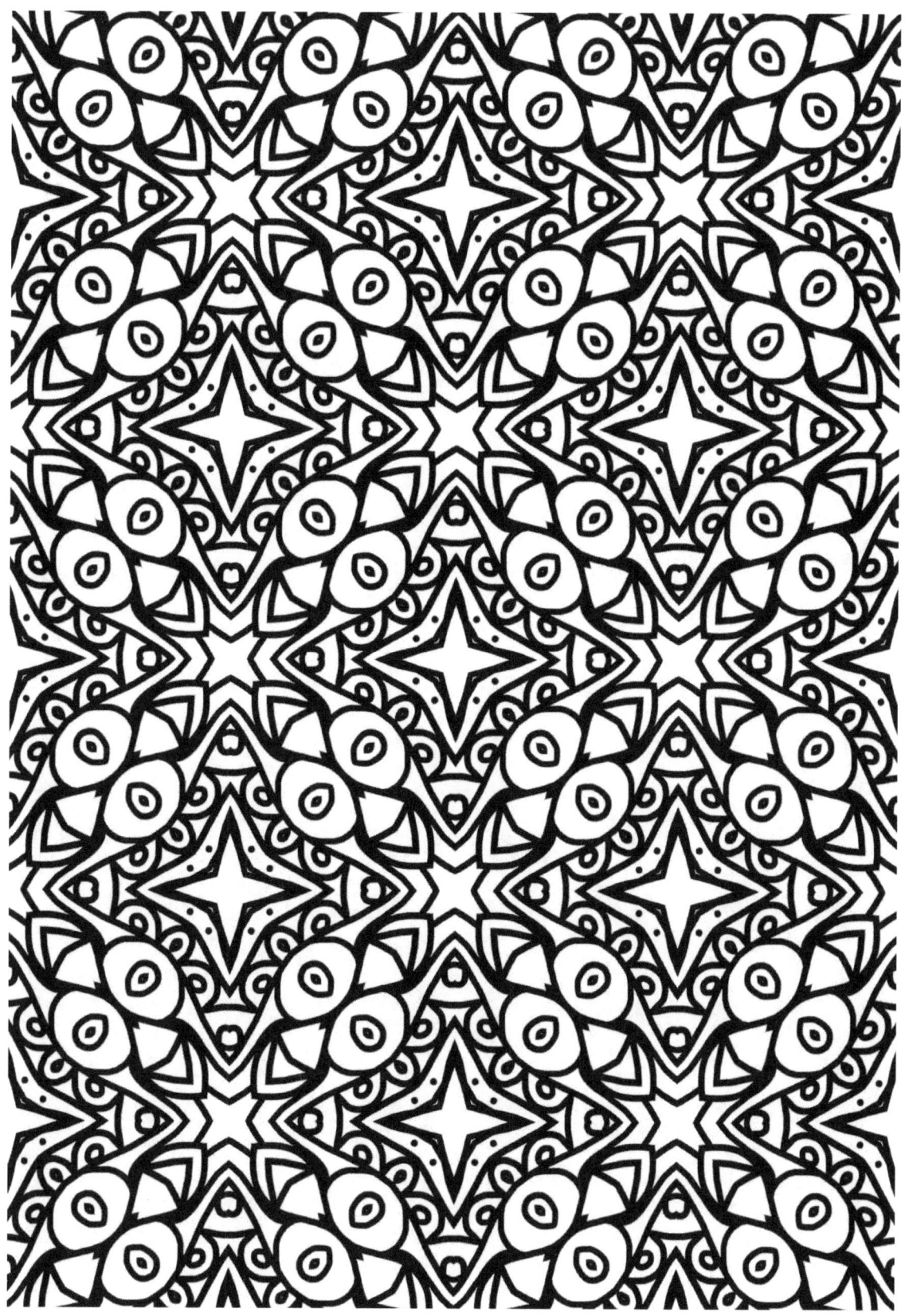

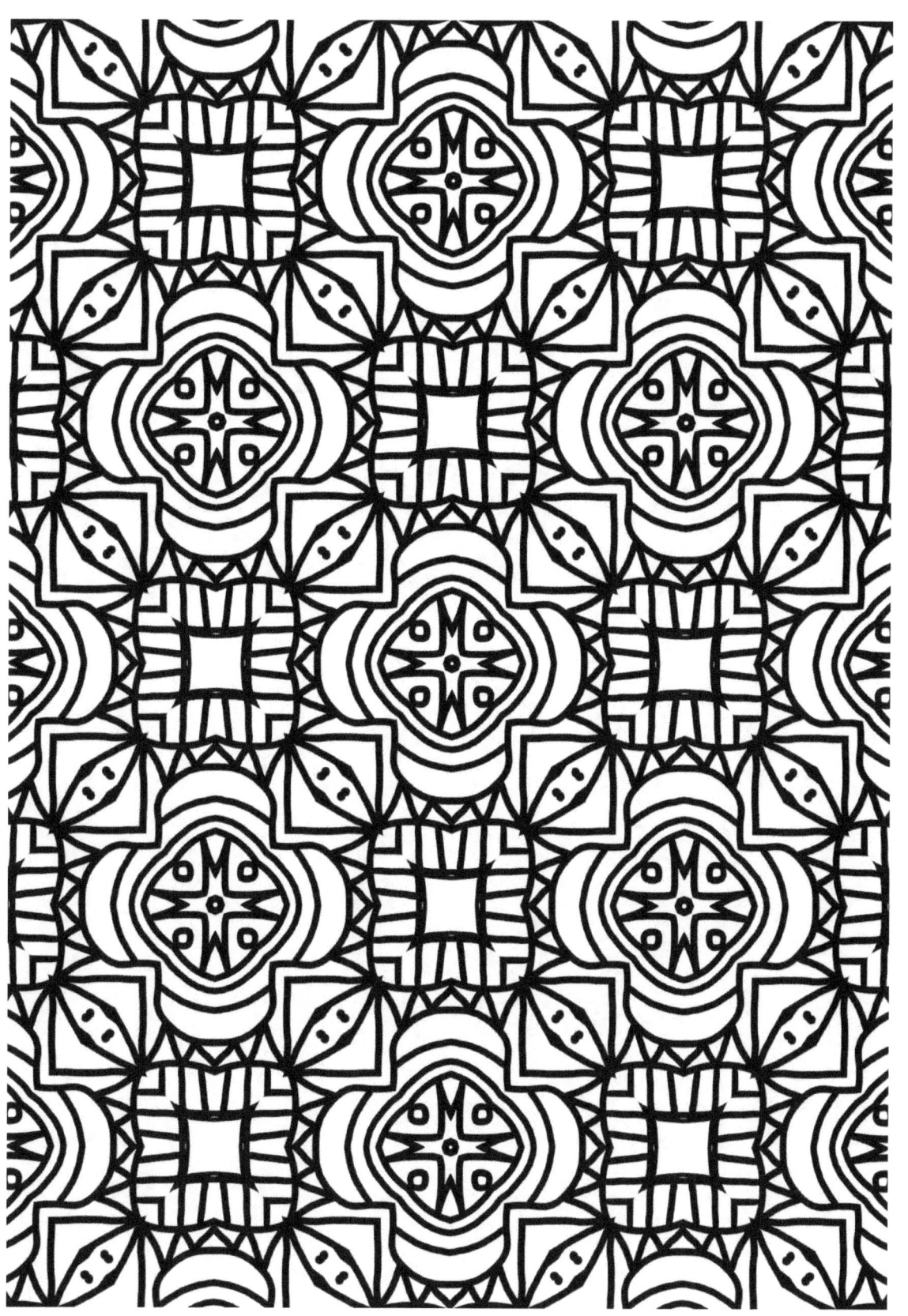

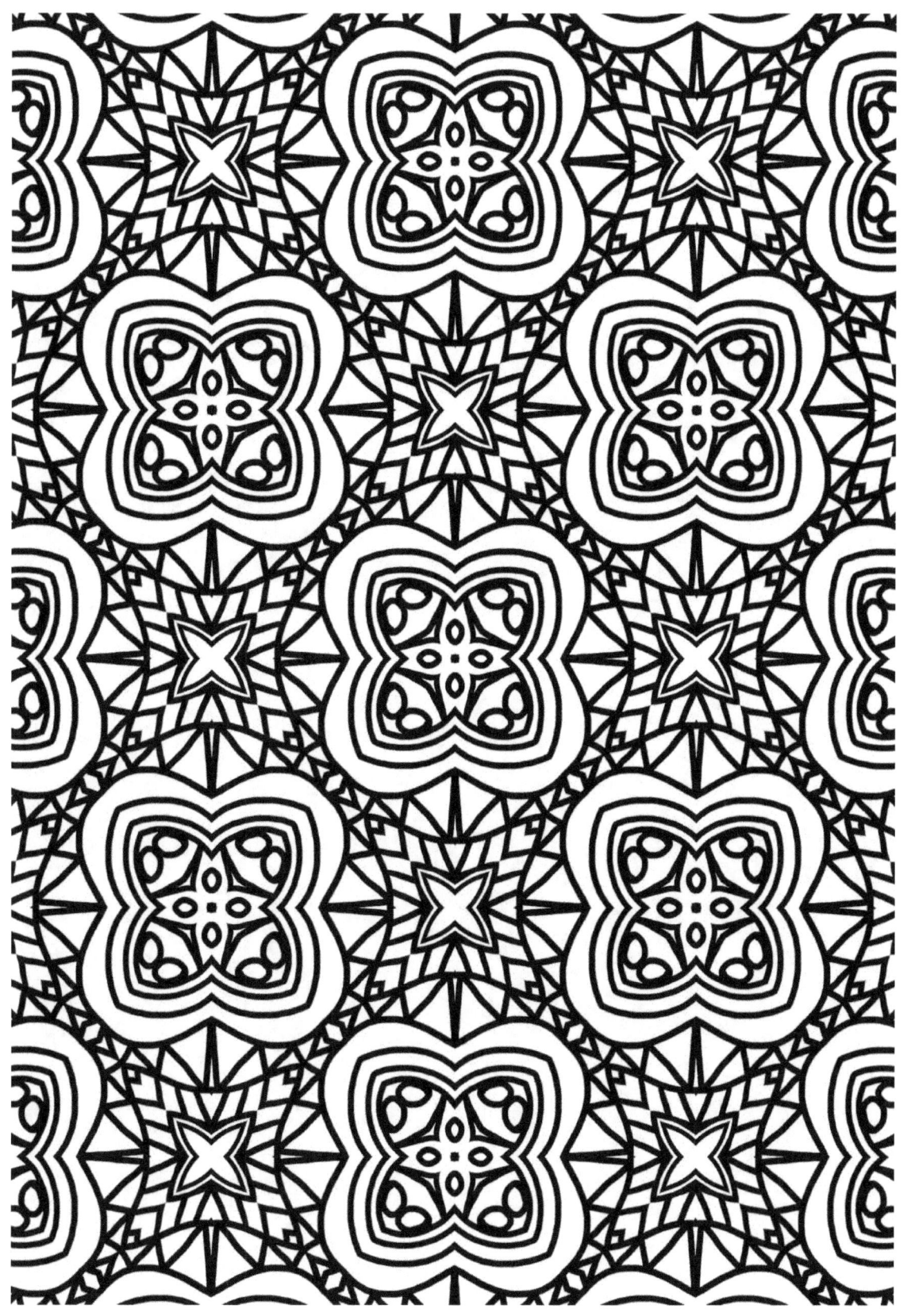

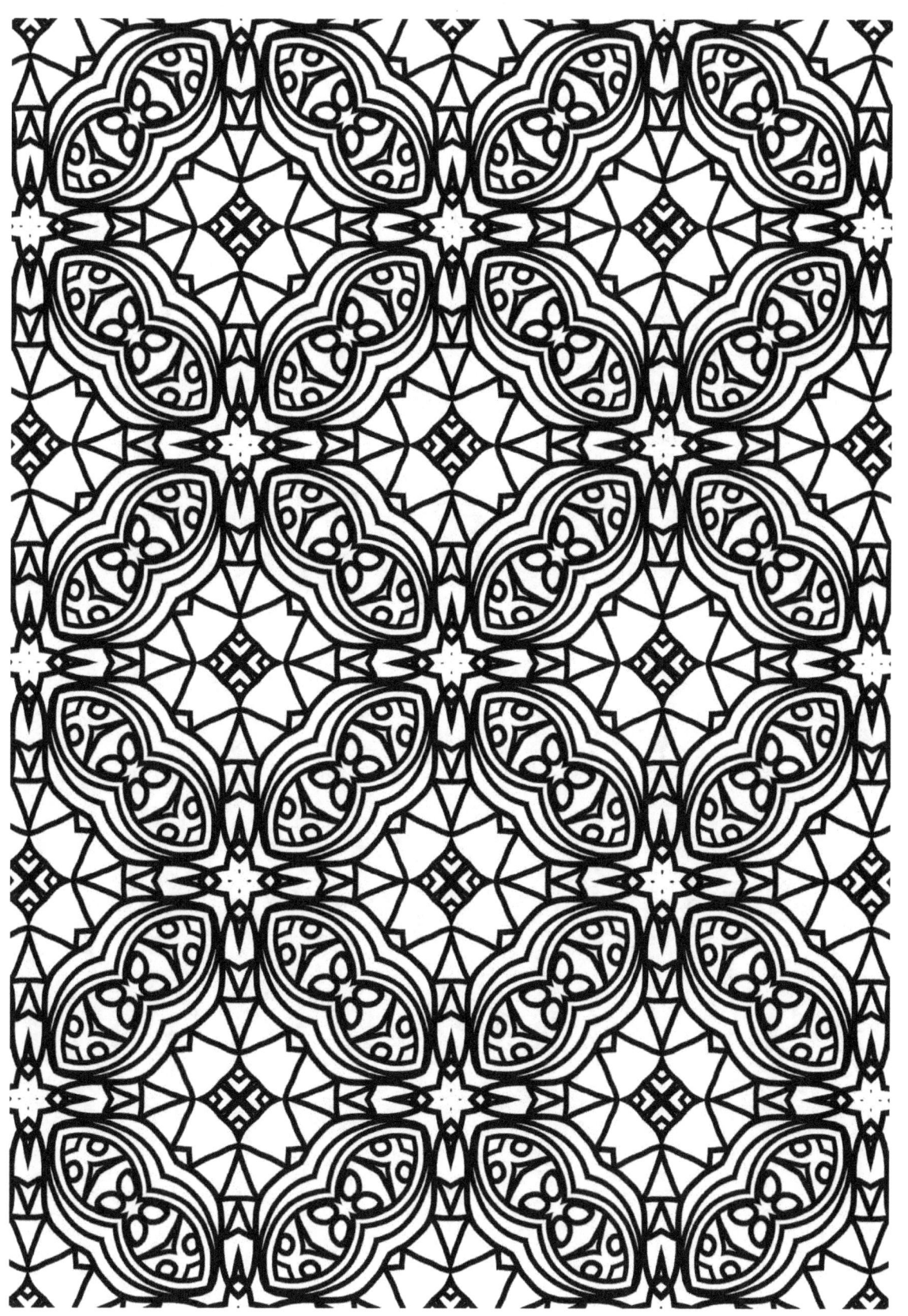

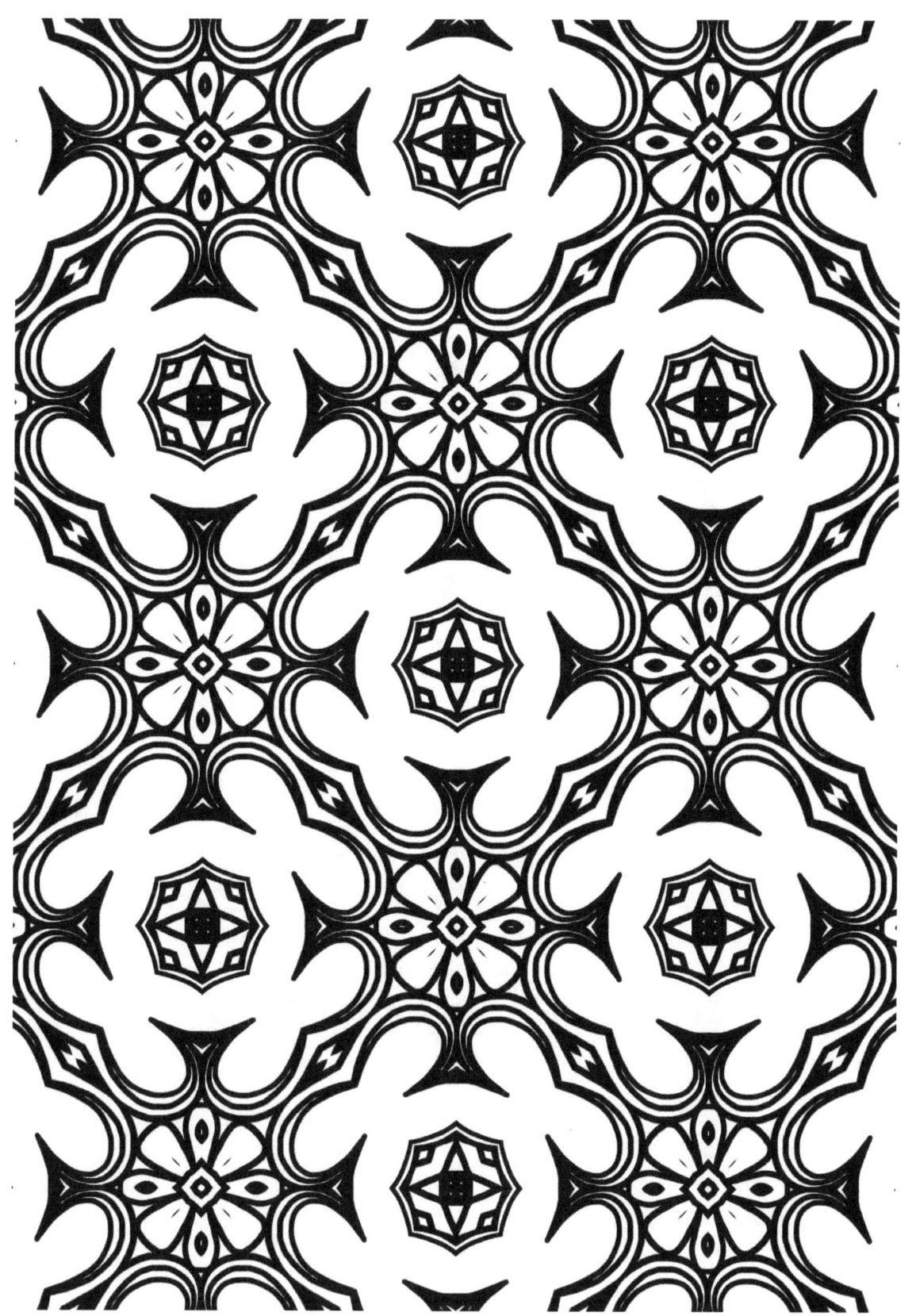

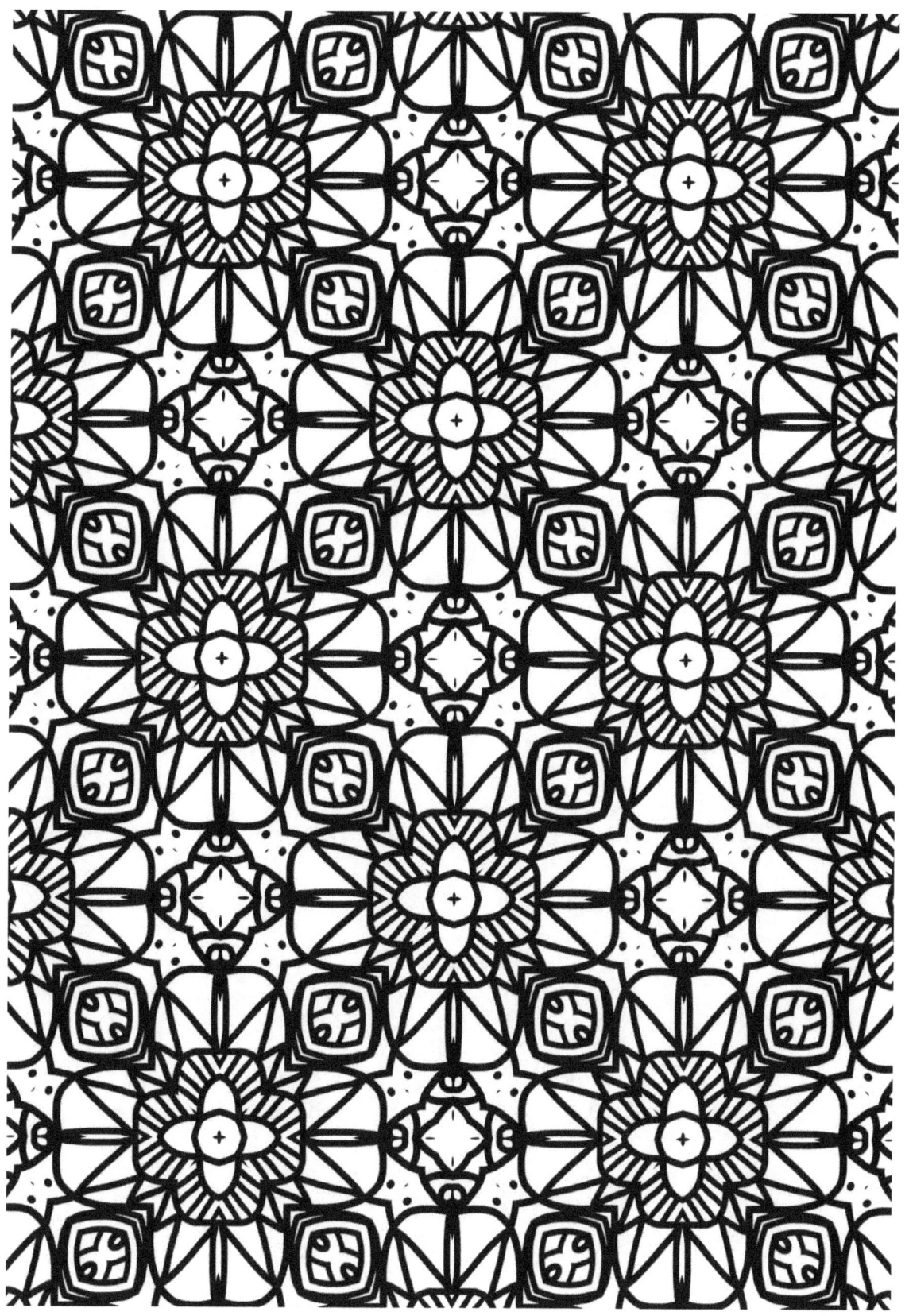

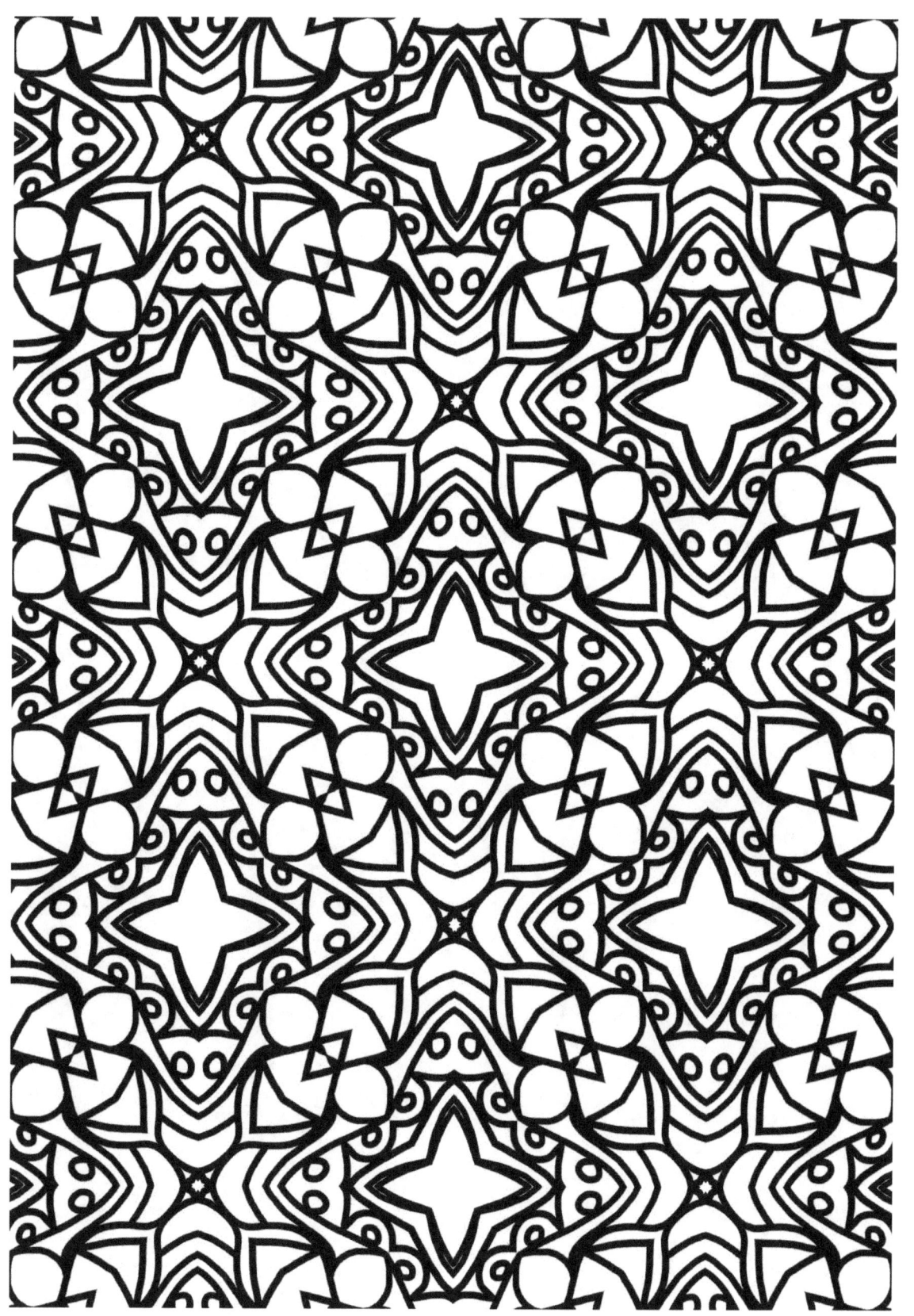

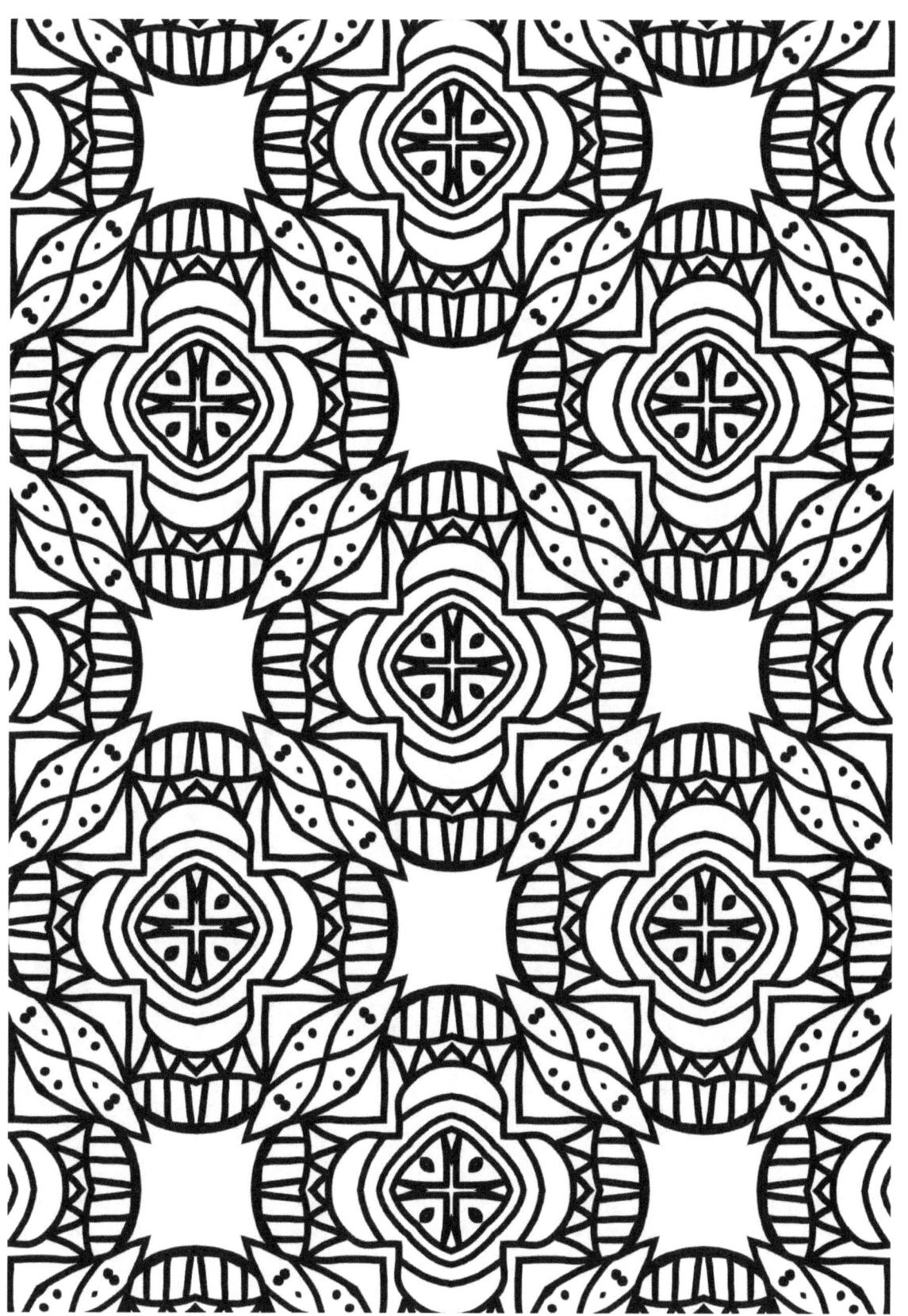

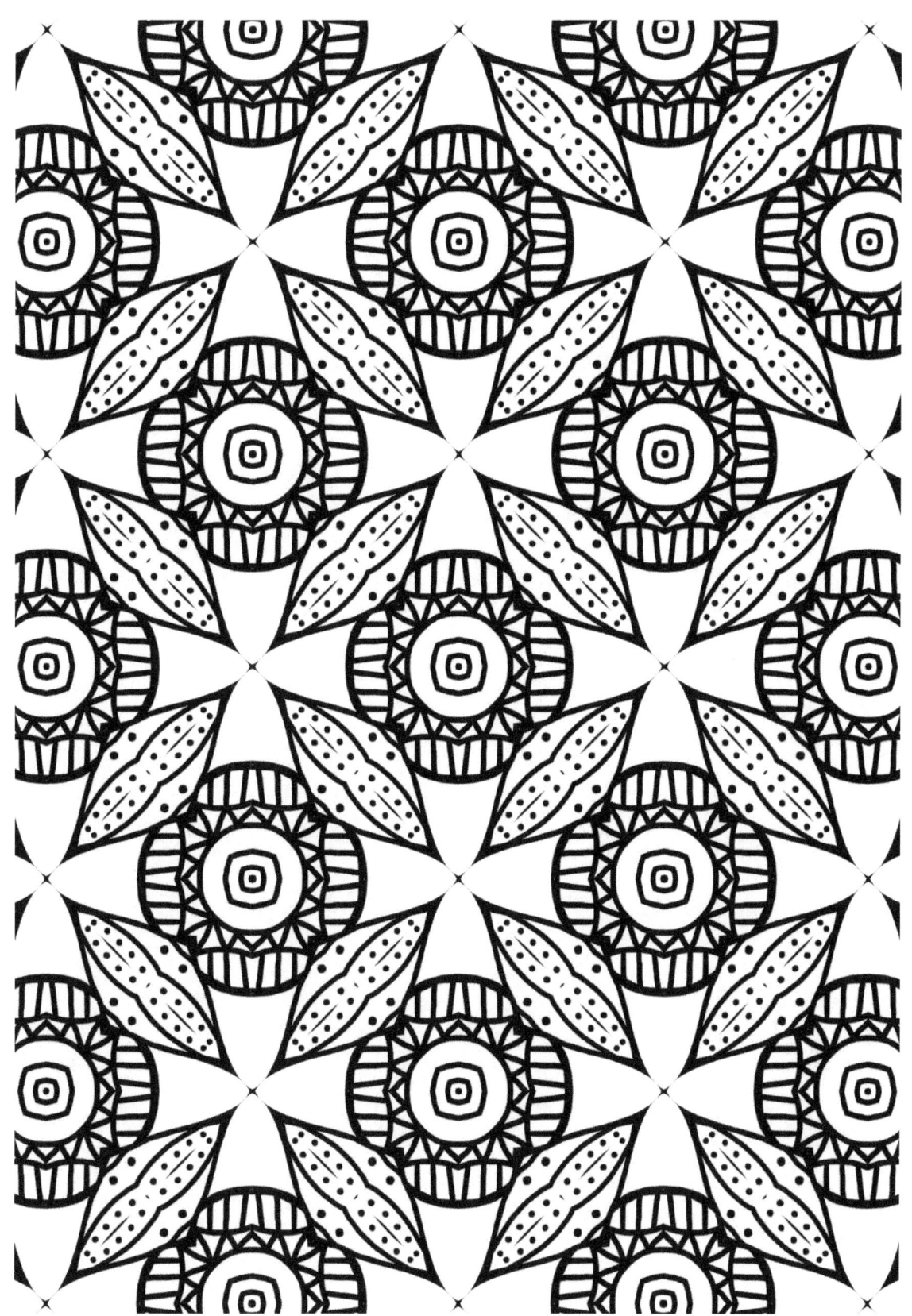

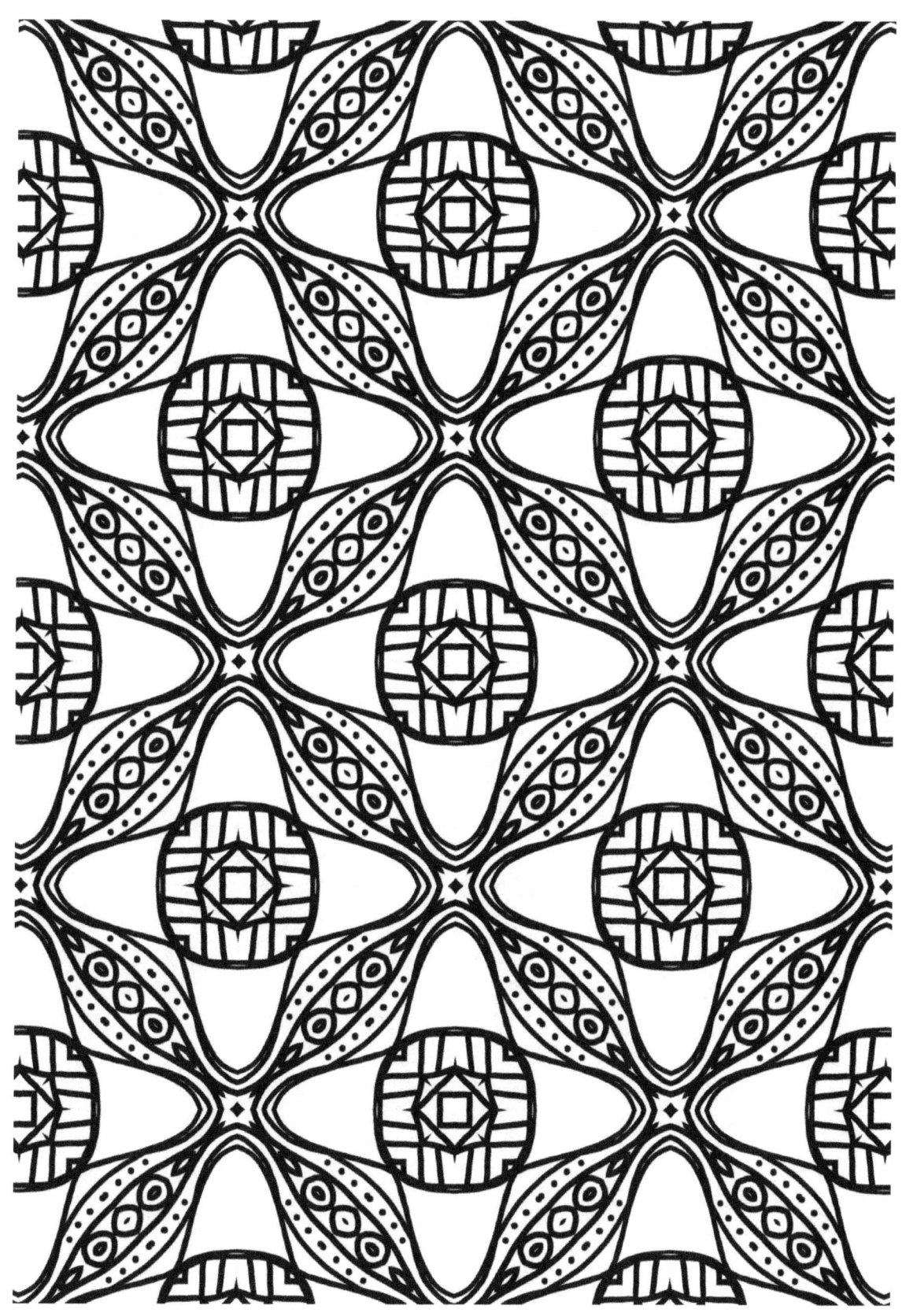

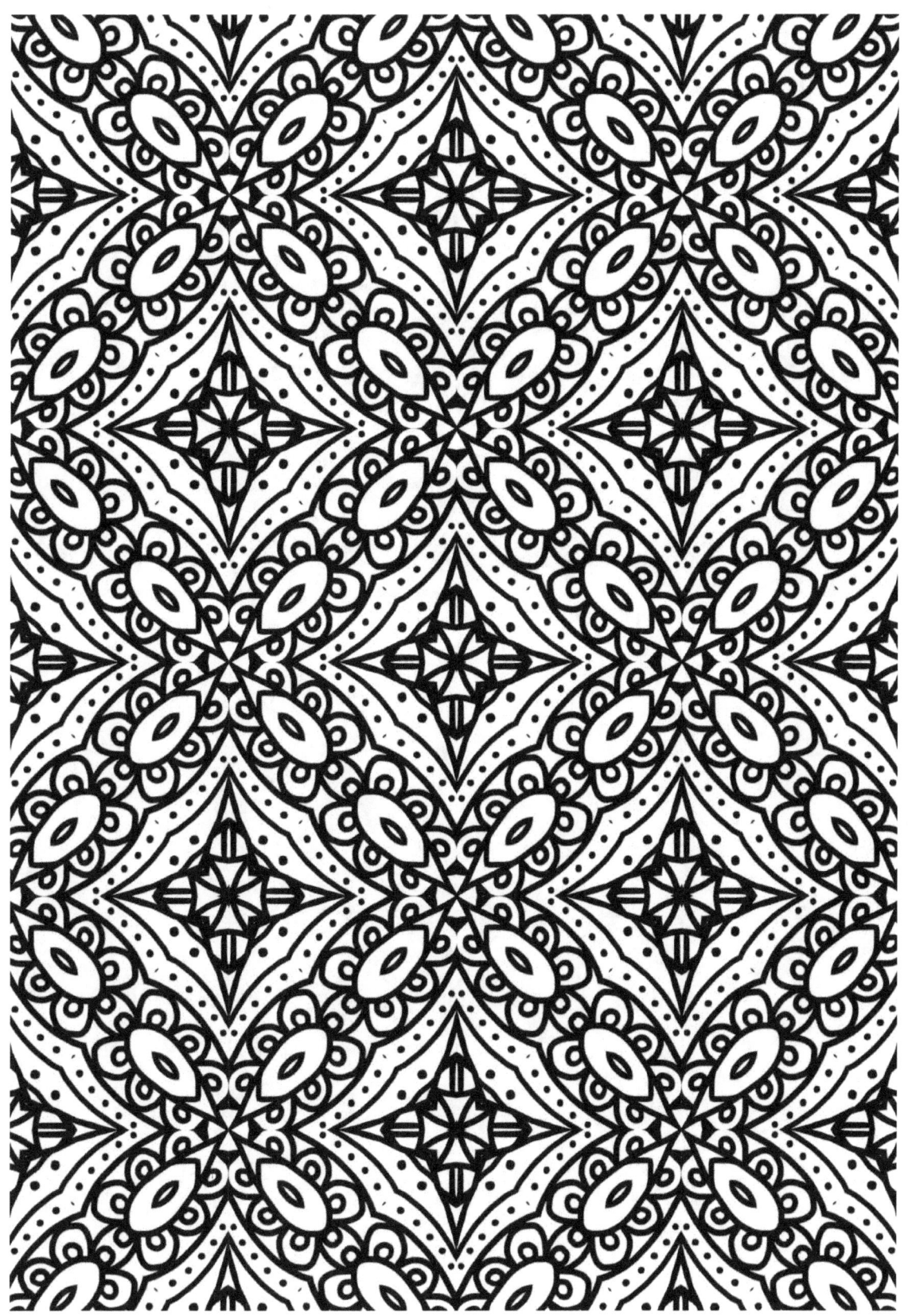

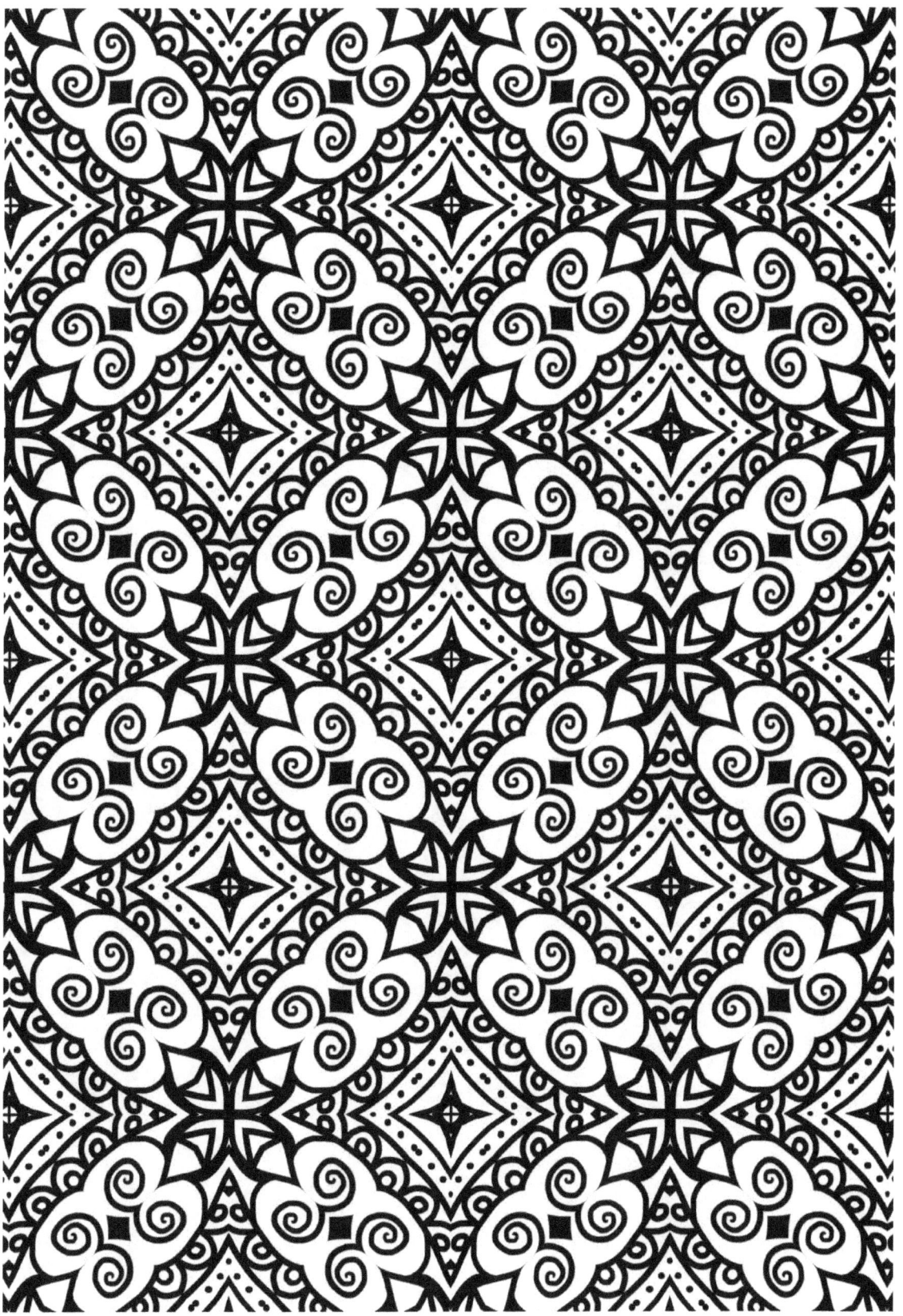

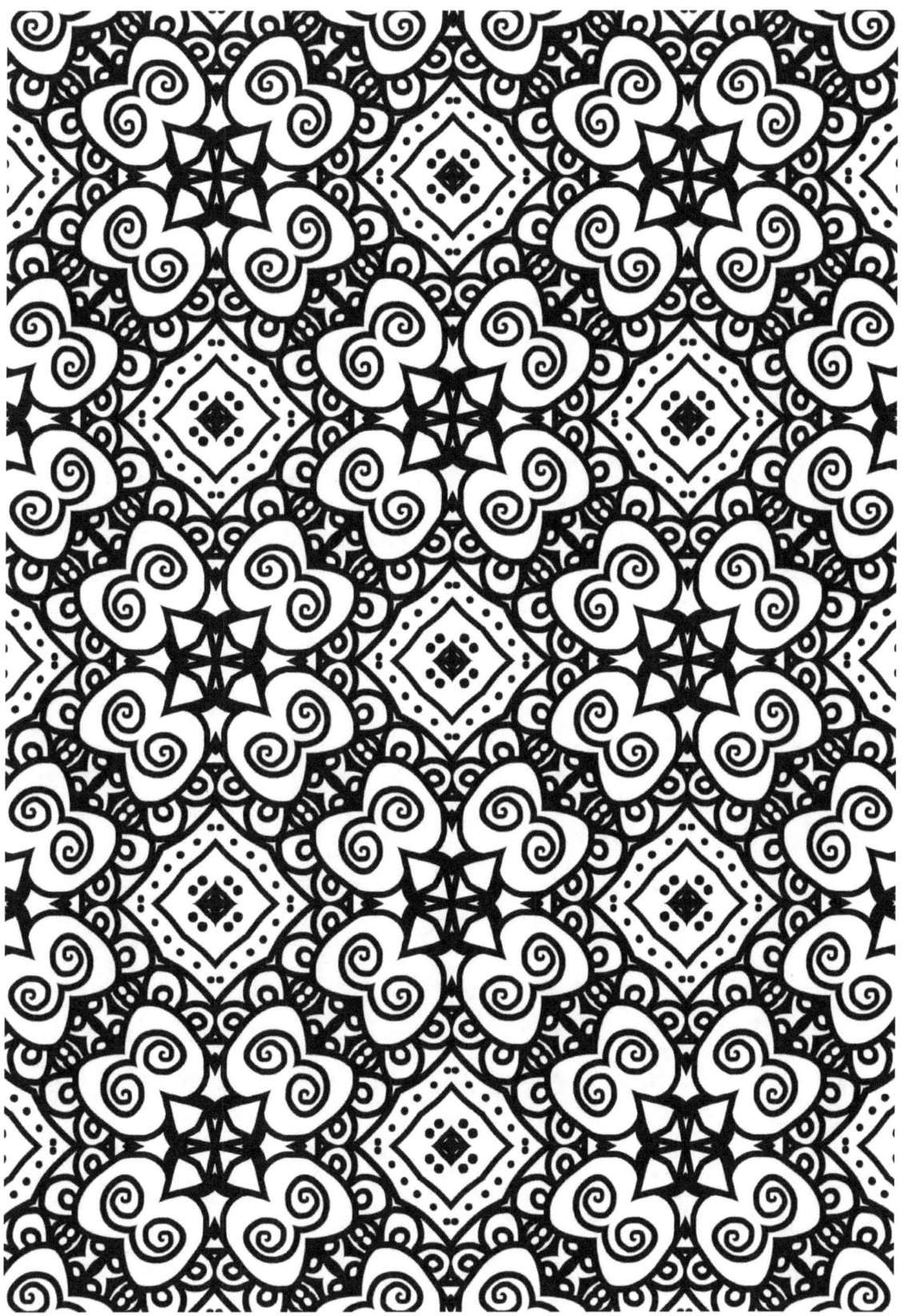

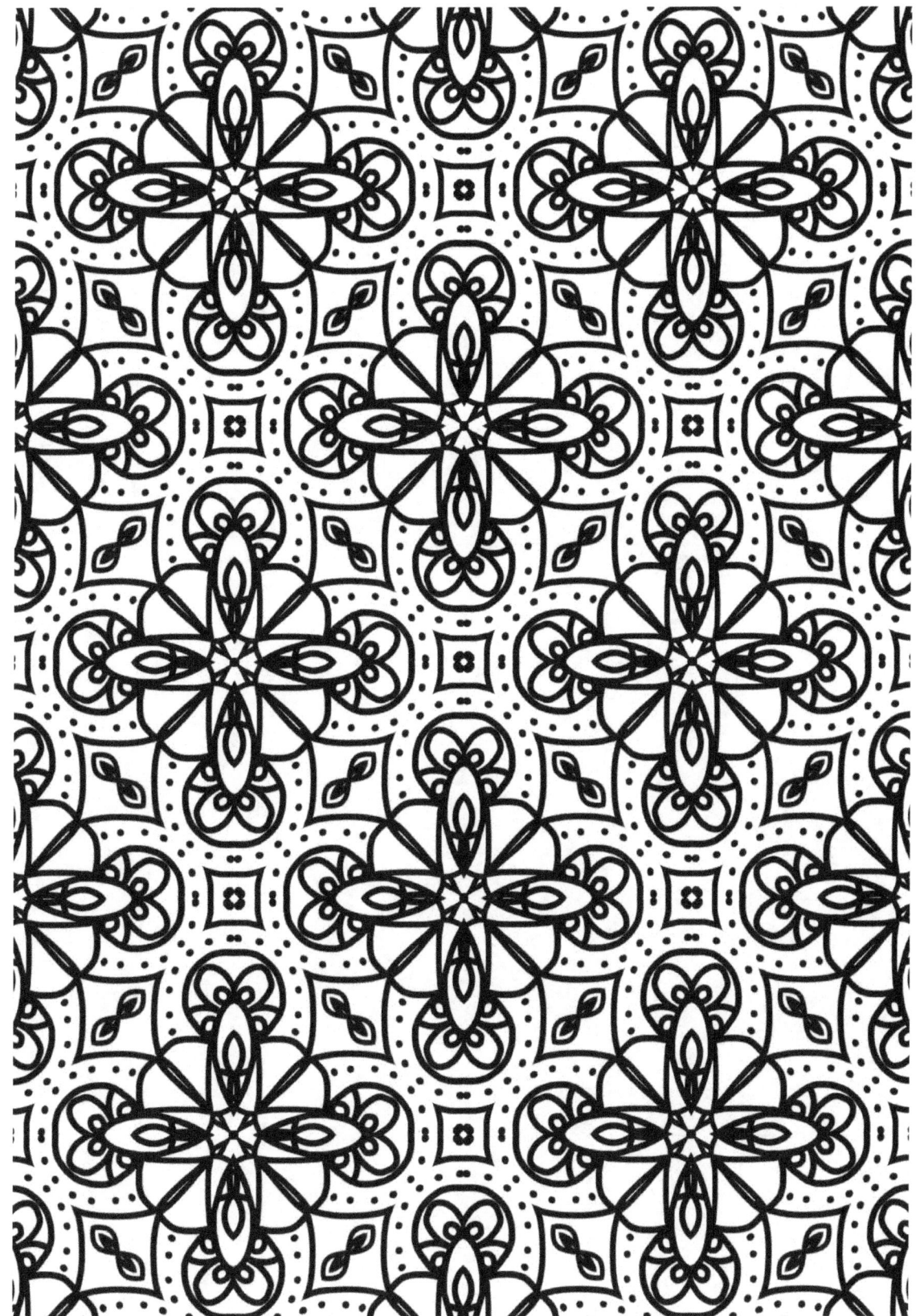

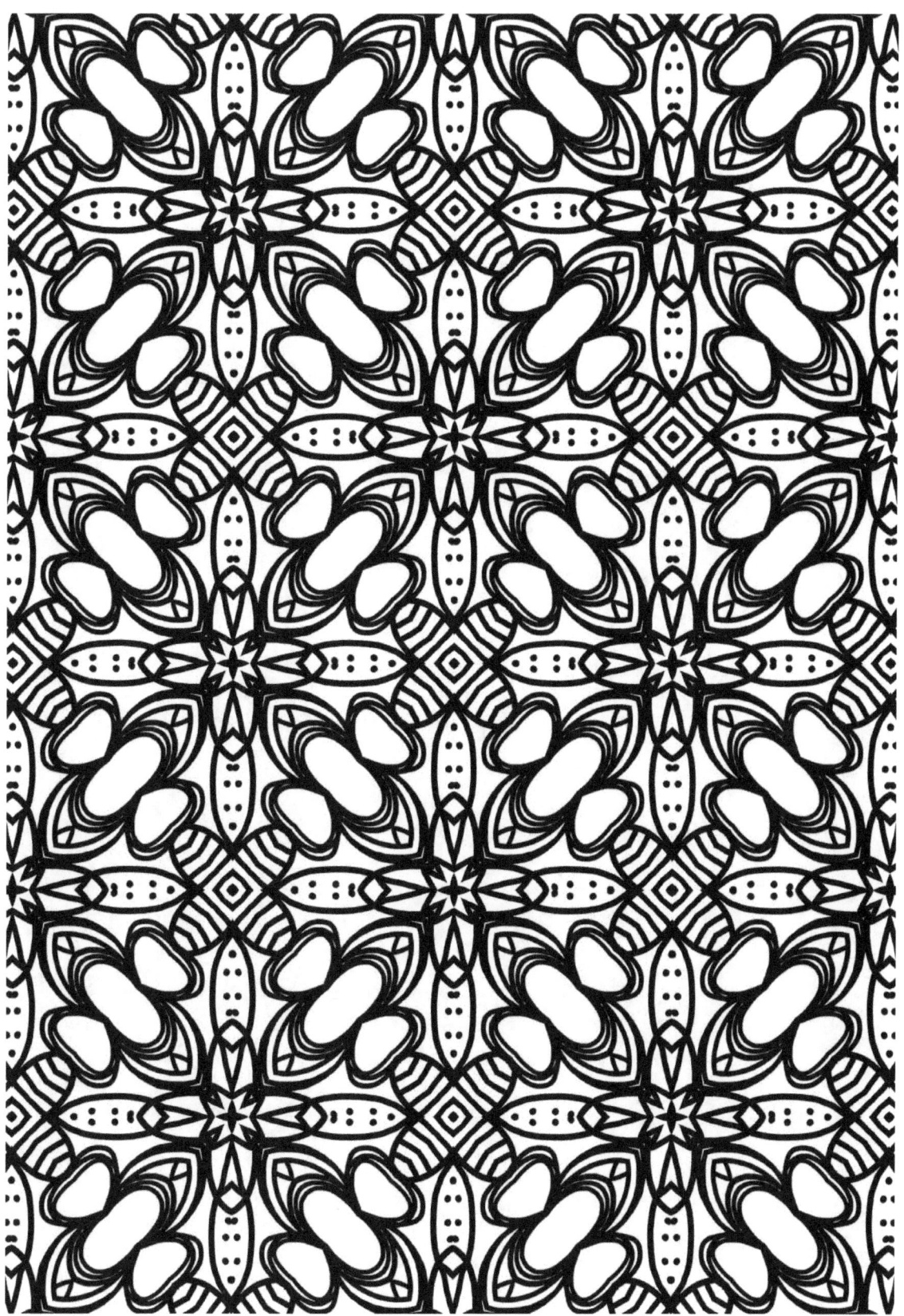

Thank you once again for purchasing my colouring book, I hope you found colouring in the designs very calming and therapeutic.

Please check out my web site:

www.colourtocalm.com for more of my colouring books

or my facebook page:

http://goo.gl/gHL0Se

or my pintrest page:

www.pintrest.com/colourtocalm

or my twitter page:

www.twitter.com/colourtocalm

Copyright © 2016 Anthony Falzon

All rights reserved. No portion of this book may be reproduced mechanically, electronically or by any other means, including photocopying without written permission of the publisher.

www.ingramcontent.com/pod-product-compliance
Lightning Source LLC
Chambersburg PA
CBHW080632190526

45169CB00009B/3372